You're the Cook!

A guide to mixing it up in the kitchen

by Katie Wilton

Layout and Cover Design:
Brown & Company Design
Portsmouth, NH 03801
www.browndesign.com

Photography: Bill Truslow Photography
Food Stylist: Trish Dahl
Make-up Artist: Lynne Avallone
Recipe Tester: Julia Grimaldi
Student Models: Carolyn S., Chelsea F., Marc F., Nick V.,
Nora C., Sam T., Sayo F.

For more information about Katie, her cooking classes
and her cookbook, please contact:

Katie
Cooking with Katie, Inc.
P.O. Box 773
Middleton, MA 01949
www.cookingwithKatie.com

Published by: Cooking with Katie, Inc.
www.cookingwithkatie.com

Photography by: Bill Truslow Photography
www.truslowphoto.com

ISBN 0-9776032-0-2
Cookery   Education

Printed in the United States of America
by Vermillion, Inc.
www.vermillion-inc.com

cooking
with Katie

A Note from Katie

This cookbook is a dream come true for me.

Ever since I had my "lightning bolt" moment when I decided to combine my love of teaching middle school students with my love of cooking, I knew cookbooks for tweens would be in my future.

This cookbook is designed to teach you where food comes from and how to cook with it. It is my goal that you will learn basic culinary skills while preparing these recipes and you will gain confidence in yourself to adjust the recipes to make them your own.

I also hope that you will take advantage of the power of cooking. It is a life skill that helps you to "do for others". Cooking provides the opportunity to gather family and friends to share stories, laughter, and ideas over a delicious meal.

Katie & her English bulldogs Putty, Dozer & Atticus
Photo by Heather Bohn-Tallman

It is time to reclaim the joys of preparing a meal and eating together so we can once again savor food – its taste, texture, and power to nourish our bodies.

Cook with Confidence!

- Katie Wilton, CCP

Table of Contents

Eggs

Berries

Cheese

Pasta

You're the Cook!

This book belongs to _____

Cook with confidence!

— Katie

Trust your palate!

Experiment!

Make it your own.

cooking with Katie

Thank you!

This book is dedicated to
Mary Devine,
my first culinary instructor.

*Katie (12 years old)
& Mary Devine*

Thank you to...

My parents for all of their support, advice, and for believing in me!

APW – for everything

Lucy RN, CPhT for editing and tasting recipes

FSW and his family JBW, FHW, SSW – and BWW, P,P,P for their encouragement

Julia Grimaldi – my friend, the recipe tester – and thank you for your culinary expertise

Andrea Cairns, Nancy Evans and the staff at Brown and Company Design

Bill Truslow and Claudia Kaerner

Trish Dahl – Food Stylist

Lynne Avallone – Make-Up Artist

Attrezzi Fine Kitchen Accessories – Photo Shoot Location
78 Market St. Portsmouth, NH 03801
www.attrezziNH.com • info@attrezziNH.com • 603-427-1667

My friends across the country and world

AND to all the 9 – 14 year old consultants –
your input was so valuable!

Common Knowledge
in the Kitchen

Dress to Cook: It is important to wear the proper attire while cooking. Shoes, an apron, sleeves rolled up, hair pulled back and no dangling jewelry are the standard.

Wash Your Hands: Clean hands are one of the best ways we can prevent diseases and illnesses passing from one another. It is very important to wash your hands after working with raw meats, eggs, and seafood. This means that you will wash your hands multiple times while preparing a meal.

Clean Up: Cooking involves several steps and one of the most important steps is cleaning up. If possible, it is best to clean up as you cook.

Oven and Stove: Common sense around these heat sources is a must.

Here are a few tips:

• keep towels, oven mitts and sleeves away from heating elements

• keep handles of pots and pans away from the edge of the stove top

• use a dry oven mitt for hot handles and for removing hot pans from the oven

• open lids away from your face, steam can also burn, and be careful when opening the oven – your eyelashes will curl up from the heat!

cooking with Katie

Knowing the ins and outs of the kitchen will make cooking fun and safe

Using Knives: Take your time when chopping and cutting. Keep fingers back, tips down and place dirty knives to the side of the sink, not in soapy water. A grater is as sharp as a knife so the same rules apply.

Cutting Boards: Having designated cutting boards just for raw meat products is a great way to prevent cross-contamination. I use my blue and pink cutting boards for raw meats and everything else is prepared on white cutting boards. Always wash boards with warm water and soap between uses or clean in the dishwasher.

Communicate: When you are cooking and there are other people in the kitchen, you need to communicate especially when you are removing a pot from the stove or a hot pan from the oven. Let people know where you are so they do not bump into you and get burned.

Cook Responsibly: It is best to get permission from an adult before cooking. Cooking with others can make the whole experience more enjoyable and it is nice to know someone is there to help you if you need it.

CooKnowledge™

The following are some tips and techniques to help you when preparing the dishes in this cookbook.

1. 'Mise en Place'
Everything in its Place:

One of the keys to success when executing a recipe is a process called 'Mise en Place' which translates to Everything in its Place.

Here's how it works...

- Begin cooking with a clean kitchen and work space.
- Read the recipe through a couple of times.
- Gather all cooking supplies needed. Preheat oven.
- Collect and prepare all ingredients including measuring, chopping, grating, slicing, etc.
- Clean as you go!

By following these steps you will make sure you have all of the supplies and ingredients required; ingredients will be prepped and ready when needed for each step in the recipe.

2. Measuring: There are two types of measuring cups.

One is designed for liquids and the other for dry ingredients. It is important to measure ingredients accurately because it can affect the success of the recipe.

tablespoon

teaspoon

When measuring liquids, always place the cup on a flat surface and make sure the liquid lines up properly with the correct measurement line.

When measuring dry ingredients – especially flour – always pour the flour into the measuring cup and then use a flat-edged utensil to sweep off the excess, creating an even surface.

cooking with Katie

Culinary techniques that are essential to the success of each recipe you make

③ Knife Skills & Chopping: You should work with knives that are sharp. You should hold your knife close to the blade as shown in the photograph.

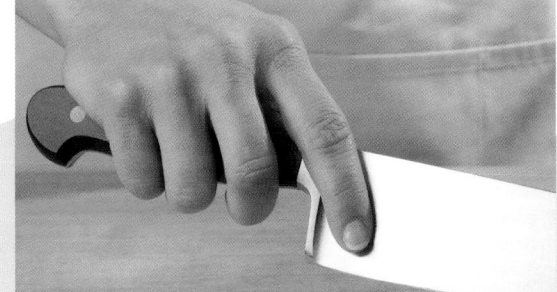

Scissors can also be used to chop herbs, trim fat from chicken breasts or to slice scallions.

There are different styles of cutting and chopping: minced, small chopped, large chopped, sliced, julienne.

minced   small chopped   large chopped   sliced   julienne

④ Securing a Cutting Board: When cutting on a cutting board it is important to make sure that the board does not slide around on the counter. Place a damp towel under the cutting board to secure the surface.

⑤ Piping Fillings: Pastry bags or the corner of a sealed bag are both great for piping fillings. Fold down the top of the bag, place the filling inside close to the tip, unfold the top, twist and then cut off the tip with a pair of scissors. This is a great trick to make it look as if a professional did it. The best part is that when you are finished, you can simply throw the sealed bag away!

6 Seasoning: Almost every recipe has the phrase "salt and pepper to taste". Some people like pepper while others do not. The general rule is to add 1/4 of a teaspoon to begin with then taste and adjust seasoning if necessary. The key is… do not add too much salt and pepper because you can always add more, but you can not take it away!

7 Tasting: Be sure to taste what you have made to check for proper seasoning, temperature and taste. It is at this time that you can make adjustments to make the dish perfect! Designate one spoon that you use to dip into the dish and pour the contents onto another spoon that you place in your mouth. No double dipping!

8 Alternatives/Substitutions: The recipes in this book make reference to full fat dairy products and butter because they have the richest flavor. You may substitute with lower fat milks and cheeses. Olive oil or light cooking sprays can be a substitute when sautéing or frying.

9 High Altitude Cooking: Recipe testers in Denver, CO reminded me that cooking times for boiling pasta and the cooking time for boiling eggs is longer because of the higher altitude.

10 Using the Best and Freshest Ingredients: The quality of the ingredients does make a difference! It is best to select the best produce and the freshest ingredients when shopping. Check expiration dates. Spices and baking powder only last a year so it is a good idea to date these items when you purchase them.

Salt

Salt is a mineral, sodium chloride (NaCl), 40% sodium and 60% chloride. Both play important roles in the human body. Sodium regulates the exchange of water between cells while chloride aids in the digestive acid in the stomach and enables the blood to carry carbon dioxide. Salt enters our bodies through the foods we eat. While some foods naturally have salt in them, salt is added to foods to enhance flavors and it reduces bitterness.

There a several types of salt –

- **Table salt**: finely ground salt used for cooking and as a table condiment but lacks iodine

- **Iodized salt**: table salt with the addition of iodine.

- **Kosher salt**: a larger grain salt with no additives and a milder flavor

- **Sea Salt**: a salt product from the evaporation process; large granules that are not easily dissolved

Before refrigeration salt was used as a preservative for meats and is a key ingredient in pickling. It is estimated that each person around the world consumes between 6-9 grams of salt a day.

Where does salt come from? There are two common methods used to cultivate salt: solar evaporation and rock salt mining. Solar evaporation makes use of the seawater that covers most of the world. It is said that for every 1,000 pounds of salt water, 35 lbs of it is salt. Salt water is collected in shallow ponds and the water evaporates with help from the sun. The concentrated salt water is placed into another pond where is begins the crystallization process and, when it is ready, a mechanical harvesting machine collects the salt crystals.

The rock salt mining method requires large chunks of the salt mineral to be mined from the earth and it is ground into particles. Because salt is a mineral, it has an infinite shelf life.

Pepper

Pepper comes from a peppercorn which is a berry that is dried and then ground into the spice that is widely used around the world. The pepper tree is a shrub that likes to climb other trees and can reach a height of over 33 feet. Favoring hot and humid climates, pepper trees grow in tropical regions. India is the main producer followed by China, Indonesia and Brazil. White flowers first appear in groups of 150 florets. These flowers hang down on what looks like a spike. The flowers then ripen into berries; a process that takes place three years after a pepper tree has been planted. A pepper tree will produce berries for another 6-7 years.

Peppercorns come in three different colors: black, white and green. The black is picked when the berry is not quite ripe and as it dries the skin turns black. The white peppercorn is a ripe berry and its skin is removed before the drying process. White pepper is usually used for appearance purposes when black specks are not desirable in a dish. The green is a soft, under-ripened peppercorn and has a less pungent flavor. Pepper, in general, will offer a better flavor to a dish if it is freshly ground in a pepper mill. Stored in a cool, dark place, peppercorns will last one year. Ground pepper will only last 4 months.

Cream Cheese

Cream cheese is referred to as one of the mildest of all cheeses. It is made from pasteurized (process of heating milk for about 15 seconds to destroy potentially harmful

bacteria) whole milk with cream added. It is made by separating the curd from the milk with the use of a culture or rennet. The resulting soft cheese is then drained for 2-3 hours. It is then pressed for another 2-3 hours and cream cheese is made. It is important to keep cream cheese well wrapped in the refrigerator so that it will not dry out or take on the flavors of other foods in the refrigerator.

The inventor of cream cheese is unknown, but in 1872, American dairymen tried to recreate a French cheese and the result was cream cheese. Philadelphia® cream cheese was introduced in 1880 and named after Philadelphia, a city known for its dairy products. Cream cheese is spread on bagels, used in dips and is the key ingredient in cheesecake.

Basic food products that are ingredients in many recipes

Vanilla

Vanilla is one of the most popular flavorings used in cooking. It is used in both baking, for cookies, cakes, and custards, and savory cooking, to balance sauces. Vanilla, in pod form, is found in tropical climates. Mexico, Tahiti and Madagascar are the top three countries that produce this product. Vanilla pods are greenish-yellow long pods that grow on a specific orchid plant. The fruit of the plant is the pod or "bean" and is picked before it ripens. These pods are then exposed to hot steam before they are left to ferment. The process takes about 4 weeks and causes the pods to turn black. Some recipes call for the use of the pods which are usually sliced and the seeds inside are scraped out into the dish. Vanilla is most commonly used in an extract form. This is a liquid that is created by chopping the pods, soaking them in an alcohol water mixture and then it is aged. For the best results, pure vanilla extract should be used rather than imitation vanilla. Both vanilla extract and vanilla beans should be stored in a dark place but not in the refrigerator. The beans should be moist and pliable and can last up to 6 months if stored in an airtight container. A white powder might form on the beans which is natural. A one inch section of a vanilla bean is equal to one teaspoon of pure vanilla extract.

Eggs

Eggs are one of nature's most amazing food products used in both baking and savory cooking. Eggs can be prepared on their own – scrambled, fried or even cooked in their own shell. They are an essential ingredient for many recipes providing color, enrichment and structure.

Most of the eggs we eat today come from a hen, a female chicken. A hen begins laying eggs when she is 3-months-old and will lay eggs every 27 hours during her lifetime. The eggs we eat and use for cooking are not fertilized and therefore cannot become chicks. An egg is fertilized only when a rooster is present among hens.

FUN FACT: To remove a piece of shell from egg liquid simply use half of the egg shell itself to scoop it out! The shell attracts the loose piece for easy removal.

What hens eat and where they live play a major role in the composition of an egg. There are various species of chickens and this accounts for different egg shell colors. Traditionally, hens live in what are known as hen houses. These houses provide "hatching" stations, food, water and, ideally, an open area to the outdoors. Chickens must be kept in cool and ventilated conditions because they do not have sweat glands and cannot expel heat.

Eggs have 3 different parts:

Shell: A hard, protective coating varying in color typically white or brown. The shell is made up of calcium carbonate crystals and is usually not eaten.

Yolk: The yellow/orange round center is the major source of cholesterol and fat, as well as some protein, iron and vitamins A and D. The color of the yolk depends entirely on the hen's breed and diet.

White (Albumen): The white part of the egg contains half of the protein and water. It looks opaque, but when cooked, turns white. When beaten vigorously, egg whites turn into a foamy product used in dishes including soufflés, angel food cake and waffles.

Nutrition:
Eggs are a good source of high quality protein, essential vitamins and minerals. Recent research has shown that eggs are a good source of eye-healthy Lutein. Today, a number of eggs are fortified with Omega-3 fatty acids that are essential for the function of every cell in our body.

Preparation and Care:
The care of eggs requires refrigeration, and it is recommended that they be kept in their cartons because egg cartons are designed to increase the shelf life of eggs and prevent eggs from taking on refrigerator odors. Eggs will last 4-5 weeks from the date on the carton.

FUN FACT:
When whipping up egg whites absolutely no yolk can be present or the whites will not whip up!

A very common mistake made when cooking eggs is overcooking. It is important to remember that when eggs are cooked and are put on a plate, they will continue to cook. It is best to slightly undercook the eggs in the pan so that when they are placed on a plate, they will continue to cook to the perfect temperature and texture.

Uncooked eggs can contain a harmful bacteria called salmonella, which can make a person very sick. Eating raw eggs is not recommended – including cookie dough!

TIP from Katie!

When following a recipe, always use eggs that are classified as "Large". It is the standard size egg used in recipes.

Superior Deviled Eggs

Serves 6

INGREDIENTS
6 eggs
1 tablespoon Dijon mustard
3 tablespoons mayonnaise
2 tablespoons bread & butter
    or gherkin sweet pickles
    – small chopped
salt/pepper to taste
Old Bay® Seasoning

This recipe is perfect when you need a last minute finger food because you typically have all of the ingredients in your kitchen.

1 Fill a 2 quart saucepan with water. Add the eggs and a pinch of salt to the water. Bring to a boil and reduce heat to a simmer. Cook for 11 minutes so the eggs are hard-boiled. Remove eggs with a slotted spoon and place in a bowl with cold water.

2 When cold enough to touch, remove shells and cut each egg in half lengthwise. Place the egg yolks in a small bowl and egg whites on a plate.

3 Add mustard and mayonnaise to the egg yolks and with a hand mixer, mix until creamy. (Add more mayonnaise if mixture is too thick.) Using a spoon, stir in the chopped pickles and season with salt and pepper.

4 Using a small spoon, fill egg whites with yolk mixture and then top off with a sprinkle of Old Bay® Seasoning. Refrigerate for about 20 minutes. Serve cold.

18 eggs

TIP from Katie!

Place yolk filling in a sealed bag. Cut off a small corner of the bag and pipe into egg whites! Toss bag for easy cleanup!

Fried Egg Sandwich

Serves 1

INGREDIENTS

1 large egg

1/2 tablespoon butter

salt/pepper to taste

slice of cheese (American)

2 slices bread or English
   muffin or bagel – *toasted*

Breakfast is the most important
meal of the day and this egg
sandwich is a very filling, nutritious
way to start your day!

Place a small frying pan over medium heat and wait until it is warm. Add 1/2 tablespoon butter and make sure it coats the bottom of the pan.

Crack the egg into the warm pan. When white part of egg turns white, crack the yolk with a spatula and spread over the top.

Season with salt and pepper. When the egg is no longer runny flip the egg and immediately put the piece of cheese on the egg. Cook for another minute and then place in between bread slices or English muffin or bagel.

TIP **from Katie!** Make your egg sandwich to go! Simply wrap it in a paper towel (to absorb the moisture) then plastic wrap or aluminum foil and take it with you!

Quiche

Serves 6-8

INGREDIENTS

9-inch prepared frozen pie crust – blind baked
3 large eggs
1 cup half & half
1 tablespoon flour
pinch of cayenne pepper
1 teaspoon salt
1/2 teaspoon pepper
1 tablespoon butter

1/4 cup onion – small chopped
(e.g. yellow onion, scallions, shallots)
1 cup vegetables – large chopped
(e.g. broccoli, peppers, asparagus)
1/2 cup meat – large chopped
(e.g. ham, cooked bacon or sausage)
1 cup cheese – shredded
(e.g. cheddar, Swiss, provolone)

Breakfast, lunch or dinner – a meal in itself! Instead of bringing a pie to a neighbor bring a quiche and he or she will thank you for it!

1 Preheat oven to 375°.
Blind bake pie crust by placing foil over the crust and then weigh it down with pie weighs or uncooked rice. Bake for 15 minutes and remove from oven. Reduce oven to 350°. Carefully remove the foil and pie weights or rice.

2 In a medium bowl whisk together the eggs, half & half, flour, cayenne pepper and season with salt and pepper. Set aside.

3 Place a large frying pan over medium heat.
When the frying pan is warm, add the butter and then the onions and vegetables. Sauté for about 2 minutes.

4 Place pie crust on a baking sheet pan. Place sautéed vegetables into empty pie crust, add the meat and cheese and spread out fillings evenly. Pour the egg mixture into the pie crust and bake for 30-45 minutes. It is ready when it begins to puff up, it turns golden brown and a knife tip comes out clean when inserted in the middle. Allow to cool for 10 minutes. Serve warm.

TIP **from Katie!** Feel free to add a tablespoon of fresh herbs or 1/2 teaspoon of dry spices to add even more flavor!

French Toast

Serves 2

INGREDIENTS
2 eggs
1/4 cup milk
1 teaspoon vanilla extract
1/4 teaspoon cinnamon
1/4 teaspoon salt
2 tablespoons butter – divided
4 slices of bread (white, wheat,
    cinnamon or raisin)
Optional – Maple syrup or fruit syrups

Once you make this breakfast treat – there is no going back! Be prepared to make it on a regular basis.

1. In a large bowl whisk together eggs, milk, vanilla, cinnamon and salt.

2. Place a large non-stick frying pan over medium high heat. When pan is warm, add 1/2 tablespoon of butter and allow to melt. Dip a slice of bread in the egg mixture and then flip it to coat both sides of the bread.

3. Place in the pan and allow to cook for about 2 minutes on each side – until both sides are brown. Repeat process with remaining butter and bread (reduce heat if bread is browning too quickly). Serve warm with syrup.

TIP from Katie! You can top this recipe off with some fresh fruit. Bananas and berries are great choices!

Frittata

Serves 5

INGREDIENTS

7 eggs

1 tablespoon butter

1/4 cup onions – small chopped
(e.g. yellow onion, scallions, shallots)

1 cup vegetables – large chopped
(e.g. peppers, broccoli, mushrooms)

1 cup meat – large chopped
(e.g. cooked bacon, sliced sausage, or ham)

salt/pepper to taste

Looking to clean out the fridge? Make a frittata and your job is half done!

1 Preheat oven to 350°.
Whisk eggs together in a medium bowl. Season with salt and pepper. Set aside.

2 Heat a 10-inch frying pan – nonstick and ovenproof – over medium heat. Add butter to the warm pan. When butter is melted, add the onions and vegetables. Cook for 1-2 minutes until the vegetables are soft.

3 Add meat to the vegetables and evenly spread out over the bottom of the pan. Reduce the heat to medium-low. Pour the eggs into the pan and cook for about 3 minutes.

4 Carefully place the frying pan in the oven and cook until the eggs are firm – about 10 minutes. Remove from oven, loosen edge with a spatula and flip onto a plate. Cut into wedges and serve warm.

 eggs

TIP from Katie!

Add more calcium to this dish by adding 1/2 cup shredded cheese (e.g. cheddar, Parmesan, Swiss)!

Your Egg Recipe Page

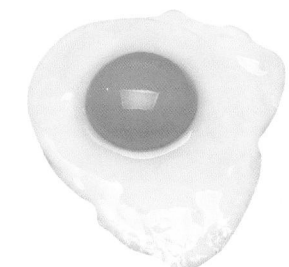

What's in your fridge? · What would happen if...? · Experiment!

Make it the way you like it! · Spice it up! · Make it your own.

Berries

Berries are small, luscious fruits that grow on bushes, shrubs or vines. They are at their peak of flavor during the spring and summer months. In the United States the strawberry is the most popular berry and the blueberry is second. The state of Maine produces about 25% of all the blueberries grown in North America and California produces over 80% of the strawberries consumed in the United States.

FUN FACT : There are approximately 200 seeds on the outside of an average size strawberry.

Strawberries

Facts:

Strawberries are a member of the rose family and are considered perennials, which mean they produce berries for two or more years. The plant grows 6-8 inches tall and spreads about one foot across. Flowers develop and then they turn into the delicious fruit that can be enjoyed fresh, frozen or in jams and jellies. Strawberries are a unique fruit because their seeds are located on the outside of the fruit. Strawberries are harvested by hand and, as a result, they are one of the most expensive fruits.

Selection and Care:

Today many markets sell strawberries year round but the best strawberries are found at your local farmer's market during their very short harvest season during the summer. When choosing strawberries always look for those that are firm, all red, and do not have white near the cap where the leaves are located. Check the bottom of the carton for any juice stains that could indicate that the berries on the bottom are mushy and moldy. Strawberries should be stored in the refrigerator and used soon after purchasing.

Strawberries (cont'd)

They should be rinsed under cold water right before eating because they will become mushy if they are washed too far in advance or if they are soaked in water. Place the rinsed strawberries on a paper towel and gently pat dry. The term hull is used to describe the process of removing the leaves (or caps) and some of the soft white core of the strawberry. This can be done with a paring knife or a melon baller.

Preparation Tips:

Strawberries freeze very well but it is best not to wash the berries before freezing. Simply spread out the berries on a sheet pan and place in the freezer. When they are frozen, place in a sealed bag. These frozen strawberries should last in the freezer for about 6-10 months.

Blueberries

Facts:

Blueberries grow on a bush and it takes 3-5 years for a blueberry bush to produce edible fruit. The bushes can grow between 5-7 feet tall and are in season from late spring to late summer. Like strawberries, they are hand picked. Harvesting takes place when the blueberries are a dark blue/purple color and have a powdery white film referred to as bloom. They should not be picked if they have a reddish tinge because they are not ripe.

Selection and Care:

Blueberries, like strawberries, should be washed right before eating and if they have a stem that should be removed. Blueberries will last up to one week in the refrigerator. Very small blueberries are normally the wild blueberries that are still found in Maine. They are very sweet and delicious!

Berries

FUN FACT: American colonists made gray paint by boiling blueberries in milk.

Preparation Tips:

When baking with blueberries, a batter is commonly used and blueberries tend to streak throughout the batter, turning it purple. This can be prevented by adding frozen blueberries to a batter at the last minute. It also helps to add blueberries to already poured batter for pancakes or waffles!
You can freeze blueberries the same way you freeze strawberries.

Nutrition:

Not only do these berries taste great, they are also very nutritious.

Strawberries are a great source of Vitamin C. One cup of strawberries has more Vitamin C than a medium orange.

Strawberries also contain fiber, folate and potassium. Both strawberries and blueberries are very low in calories. Blueberries are loaded with antioxidants which help protect our bodies from harmful particles and diseases. Eating berries raw is the best way to receive all their nutritional value.

Yogurt Fruit Shake

Serves 1

INGREDIENTS

1 cup frozen strawberries
    or blueberries
1/2 cup milk
1 cup vanilla yogurt
1 tablespoon honey

Fruit shakes are great for breakfast or a snack. You can pour it into a sealed container and drink it on the way to school.

1 Place fruit in blender followed by the milk, yogurt, and honey.

2 Blend until it is a smooth consistency adding more milk if necessary. Taste and add more fruit or honey if needed.

TIP from Katie!

You can make this ahead of time and place it in the refrigerator. The shake will separate so simply give it a stir and you are good to go! Try other berries or fruits; bananas are a great choice!

Berry Salad

Serves 4

INGREDIENTS
1 tablespoon fresh lemon juice
2 tablespoons olive oil
1/2 teaspoon Dijon mustard
salt/pepper to taste
lettuce, mesculin mix, washed/dried
6-8 strawberries, washed and sliced
1/2 cup blueberries, washed
1/4 cup walnuts – large chopped
   (toasting optional)
1/2 cup crumbled blue cheese

Some might consider that this salad is made backwards because the dressing is made first and the ingredients are added to it.

In a large bowl, whisk together the lemon juice, olive oil, mustard, salt and pepper.

Place the lettuce, sliced strawberries, blueberries and walnuts in the large bowl with dressing. Mix so that the dressing coats the fruits, nuts and lettuce.

Place on serving dishes and sprinkle with blue cheese.

TIP from Katie!

Try almonds instead of walnuts and goat cheese instead of the blue cheese to add variety to this salad.

Pork with Blueberry Sauce

Serves 4

INGREDIENTS
1/4 cup water
2 tablespoons granulated sugar
1/2 teaspoon salt
1 teaspoon fresh lemon juice
1 cup blueberries
1/4 teaspoon cinnamon
1 tablespoon butter
4 boneless pork chops (1-inch thick)
salt/pepper to taste

Blueberry sauce is a great substitute for the traditional applesauce! It adds great color and flavor to seared pork.

1 Combine the water, sugar, salt, lemon juice, and blueberries in a saucepan and place over medium low heat.

2 Allow the mixture to come to a boil. Reduce heat to low and simmer for 15-20 minutes, stirring occasionally, until it becomes a thick sauce. Remove from heat and stir in cinnamon.

3 Place a large non-stick frying pan over medium heat. Trim any excess fat from the pork chops and season both sides with salt and pepper. When the pan is very hot, add butter and then the seasoned pork chops. Sear both sides of the pork chop for 2 minutes each, then lower the heat to low. Cover pan with a lid and cook for another 5-8 minutes, turning the pork chops over at least twice. Check the internal temperature of the pork chops with a meat thermometer. The pork should be slightly pink with an internal temperature of 155°. Serve warm with blueberry sauce.

TIP from Katie! If you would like to "spice up" this dish, rub the pork chops before searing with the following rub mixture: 2 tablespoons cinnamon, 1/2 teaspoon cloves, and 1/2 teaspoon cumin.

Strawberry Coulis (Cool-ee) & Whipped Frosting

Yields about 5 cups

Dish hand-painted by Hannah Truslow

INGREDIENTS

Coulis:
16 ounce bag of frozen strawberries
1/4 cup water
1 teaspoon fresh lemon juice
1/4 cup powdered sugar

Whipped Frosting:
1 pint whipping cream
1/3 cup granulated sugar
1 teaspoon fresh lemon juice
3/4 cup strawberry coulis

This is really 2 recipes! The coulis can be used as an ice cream sauce, crêpe topping or a sauce with fruit. The strawberry whipped frosting is great on cakes, cupcakes or as a crêpe filling.

1 Place frozen strawberries and water in a saucepan and bring to a boil. Reduce heat to medium, and cook strawberries, stirring occasionally, until berries are soft and broken into pieces, about 15 minutes.

2 Remove from heat and pour into a fine sieved metal strainer and place over a medium bowl. Using a spoon, press and stir strawberries to extract the juice (this process will take about 5 minutes). Discard the seeds and thick pulp remaining in the strainer and pour the juice back into the saucepan.

3 Return saucepan to medium low heat. Allow to boil for about 10 minutes so it becomes a think syrupy sauce. Remove from heat and add lemon juice and powdered sugar. Taste and adjust flavor if necessary.

4 Cool using an ice bath (a large bowl with ice and water that you dip the saucepan with coulis in and stir sauce) or place in freezer for 20 minutes. Cool completely! Pour sauce into a measuring cup and there should be about 3/4 of a cup of strawberry coulis.

5 Place cold whipping cream and granulated sugar in a large bowl. Stir until sugar is dissolved and place bowl in refrigerator for 20 minutes. Whip with a hand mixer until cream begins to thicken. Pour in the strawberry coulis and continue to whip until it is the consistency of pudding, about 3 minutes on high speed.

TIP **from Katie!**

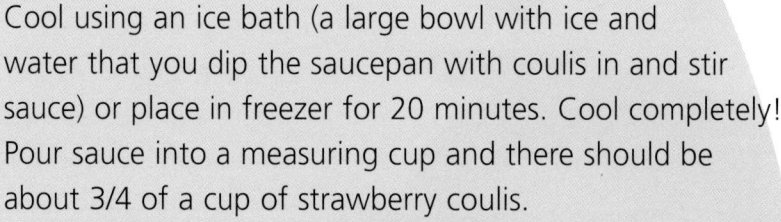

In a sealed container strawberry coulis will keep in the refrigerator for at least two weeks and six months in the freezer. It is great to have around for a last minute dessert or to use instead of maple syrup on your French toast.

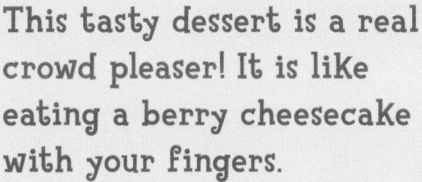

ream Cheese Filled Strawberries

Makes 12

INGREDIENTS
12 large strawberries
12 blueberries
4 ounces cream cheese
1 teaspoon fresh lemon juice
1/2 teaspoon vanilla extract
1 tablespoon honey
1 tablespoon brown sugar

This tasty dessert is a real crowd pleaser! It is like eating a berry cheesecake with your fingers.

1 Gently wash strawberries and pat dry. Remove green leaves and scoop out some of the center of the strawberries with a melon baller. Cut a bit off the bottom of each strawberry so that they will sit up on a plate. Wash blueberries, pat dry and set aside.

2 Place cream cheese, lemon juice, vanilla, and honey in a medium bowl. Mix with an electric hand mixer on medium speed until light and fluffy. Place the mixture in a pastry bag or a sealed bag to pipe filling into strawberries.

3 Pipe the cream cheese filling into each strawberry, sprinkle with some brown sugar and top with a blueberry. Serve chilled.

TIP from Katie!

These need to be made at the last minute. If you are bringing them to a party, take all the prepared ingredients, including the filling in the bag and assemble when you are just about to serve them so the strawberries do not get soggy.

Your Berry Recipe Page

Trust your palate! · Have fun with it! · Spice it up!

Be Creative! · What's in your fridge? · Try something new.

Cheese

Cheese is one of the oldest "made" foods in the world. For thousands of years, it has been made from the same basic ingredient, milk. It takes 100 pounds of milk to make 10 pounds of cheese. Today, we can find over 300 varieties of cheese in the United States alone, as well as a number of different varieties throughout Europe and Canada. Wisconsin is the #1 producer of cheese in the USA. France, Italy and Spain also produce a number of delicious cheeses that are popular in the USA.

FUN FACT : Cheese can be made from the milk of a cow, goat, sheep or water buffalo. Cheese has also been made from reindeer milk but it is rare.

The first step in making cheese begins with heating the milk, a process known as pasteurizing. An enzyme, usually rennet, is added to cause the milk to curdle. Curdling is when the whey, the liquid found in milk, separates from the casein, the white milk solids. Rennet comes from the "true" stomach of a milk-fed calf. Today, it can also come from vegetable extracts so that certain cheeses can be considered a vegetarian product. The whey is removed and the curds become firm because of the absence of the liquid. It is at this point that the basic categories of cheese separate into two major types: fresh and aged, also referred to as ripened. These categories are then broken down even further.

FUN FACT : Americans eat over a half a pound of cheese per person, per week. America's favorite cheeses are cheddar and mozzarella – think mac-n-cheese and pizza.

Salt and other ingredients are added to the curd depending on what type of cheese is being produced. The curd is then pressed and/or molded. If the cheese is to age, it is placed in an environmentally specific area where it begins its maturing process. Soft cheeses are placed in a moist environment while a dry environment aids in the hardening of firm cheeses. A common practice for some varieties of cheese is to be aged in caves or cellars. These protected enclosures provide an ideal environment where temperature and the proper humidity can be controlled. Some caves have specific molds, yeasts and/or healthy bacteria placed in them in order to create the desired cheese.

Types of cheese:

Fresh – a mild, soft un-ripened cheese, meant to be eaten fresh, e.g. cottage cheese, cream cheese

Stretch-curd – made by immersing the curds into hot water and then stretching the curds by pulling and kneading them into the final product, e.g. mozzarella and provolone

Soft-ripened – uncooked curds that firm naturally and are placed into molds and aged for a short period of time, e.g. brie, camembert

Semi-soft – cooked and not pressed, resulting in a soft texture that can be easily sliced, e.g. havarti, monterey jack, muenster

Semi-firm (semi-hard) – pressed, uncooked and aged cheeses that are firm in texture. They usually have a light yellow color, e.g. cheddar, asiago, gruyère

Firm (hard) – pressed, cooked and aged to create a hard texture. They are best for grating, e.g. parmesan, pecorino romano

Blue-veined – Soft ripened cheeses that have been injected with the spores of unique molds which create the blue "veins" and form the strong flavor and texture of blue cheeses, e.g. stilton, roquefort, maytag blue and gorgonzola

Goat's milk – mild and creamy, and the flavor sharpens with age and as it hardens. Found in various shapes but typically in logs or wheels, e.g. montrachet, crottin, chevre

Sheep's milk – firm curds that are pickled in a brine solution of salt water, e.g. feta

Selection and Care:

Cheese should be stored at a temperature between 35°-40°. It is best to keep cheese in its original packaging and it must be well wrapped in plastic wrap or dry paper or placed in a sealed bag or in an airtight container. The flavor of hard cheeses improves while it ages and can be kept in the refrigerator for 2-4 weeks or up to 10 months for parmesan cheese. Soft cheeses are made to be consumed promptly, within 7-10 days. Some types of cheese have an outer layer known as the rind. Most rinds should not be eaten, except for the white soft rind found on cheeses such as brie and camembert. Cheese is best served at room temperature. Remove it from the refrigerator at least one hour before serving.

Nutrition:

Cheese is an excellent source of calcium, Vitamin D and protein. Calcium is a mineral that is necessary for the growth of strong bones and teeth. People between the ages of 11 and 18 should consume at least 4 servings of low fat milk, yogurt or cheese everyday.

Pizza Wontons

Serves 2 (5 each)

INGREDIENTS
2 mozzarella sticks
10 thin slices pepperoni
10 round or square wonton
   wrappers
1 tablespoon olive oil
2 tablespoons water
pasta sauce

Have fun creating new fillings. One group of my students suggested peanut butter and jelly!

1 Cut mozzarella stick in half lengthwise and then cut into 1/2-inch pieces. Place the 2 tablespoons of water in a cup. Layout wonton wrappers. Place a slice of pepperoni in the middle and then place two pieces of mozzarella on top of it. Dip your finger in the water and then run your finger all around the edge of the wonton wrapper. Fold the wonton wrapper over and seal the edge by pressing down with your fingers. Set aside on a plate.

2 Place a large non-stick frying pan over medium heat. When it is warm, add the olive oil and swirl it around. Carefully place the pizza wontons in the pan. Brown for about 1 minute on each side using tongs to flip them over. Remove pan from the heat. Add remaining water to the pan, (be very careful because it will splatter) and quickly cover with a lid.

3 Let sit for 1 minute. Carefully remove cover. Place wontons on a serving plate and serve with a small amount of warm pasta sauce. Eat immediately.

TIP from Katie! Make sure you do not overfill the wontons. If you do, they will not remain sealed. Also, square wonton wrappers need to be trimmed to form an equilateral square before forming into a triangle!

Parmesan Pita Triangles

Serves 2-4

INGREDIENTS

2 pita pockets – white or wheat
4 tablespoons butter – softened
1 cup grated Parmesan
Optional toppings – pepperoni and/or chopped herbs

These will be a must whenever you have a large bowl of pasta or when you would like a quick "cheesy" snack! Our grandmother "Gram" used hotdog buns instead of pita.

1 Using scissors, cut pita pockets in half, then open the pita and separate the sides so that you have 4 semi-circular pieces.

2 Spread about half a tablespoon of butter on each semi-circle, cut in half, sprinkle with cheese and top with optional toppings.

3 Place on aluminum foil in toaster oven and toast until the cheese is melted and they are light brown. Serve warm.

TIP **from Katie!** Use non-stick foil because it prevents any cheese from sticking to the foil!

Quesadillas

Serves 2-4

INGREDIENTS

2 boneless chicken breasts
1 medium yellow onion – cut into thin strips – julienne
1 red pepper – cut into thin strips – julienne
1 green pepper – cut into thin strips – julienne
2 cups cheddar cheese or Mexican cheese mix, shredded

6 (8-inch) flour tortillas
2 tablespoons butter
2 tablespoons vegetable oil
dash of cayenne pepper
dash of chili powder
salt/pepper to taste
Optional: sour cream and salsa

This versatile dish can be a main meal or served as an appetizer or an after-school snack. If you leave out the meat your vegetarian friends can enjoy this!

1 Place a large non-stick frying pan over medium heat. When it is warm add 1 tablespoon of butter. Sauté the onion and peppers until they are soft about 3 minutes and set aside in a large bowl.

2 Trim the fat from the chicken breasts and cut the chicken into thin, short strips. Place the strips in a small bowl and season with the cayenne pepper, chili powder, salt and pepper. Mix, coating each chicken strip.

3 Replace the non-stick frying pan over medium high heat and wait until it is hot. Add the remaining 1 tablespoon of butter and sear the chicken strips turning to make sure that all sides of the chicken strips are cooked. Cook for a total of 5 minutes. Add the chicken to the bowl with peppers and onions and mix.

4 Carefully wipe the frying pan clean with two paper towels and place over medium heat. Add a tablespoon of oil to the pan and wait until it is warm. Place a tortilla in the pan and sprinkle with about 1/4 cup of cheese. Top with some of the chicken/onion/pepper mixture, sprinkle with another 1/4 cup of cheese and place another tortilla on top. Cover the pan and cook for about 1-2 minutes or until bottom tortilla is lightly brown and crisp. Carefully flip the tortilla with a large spatula and cook on the other side for 1-2 minutes. Remove from heat and cut into triangles. Serve warm with a dollop of sour cream and/or salsa.

TIP from Katie! Quesadillas can be made ahead of time and reheated in the toaster oven.

Macaroni & Cheese

Serves 5

INGREDIENTS

3 cups monterey jack cheese – shredded
3 cups cheddar cheese – shredded
1-1/2 teaspoons dry mustard
1 teaspoon worcestershire sauce
1/2 teaspoon salt

dash of cayenne pepper
pepper to taste
Optional: pinch of nutmeg
1-1/2 cups milk – divided
1/2 cup heavy cream
1 tablespoon cornstarch
3 cups dried medium pasta shells

I learned this recipe while working at a gourmet food shop in Columbus, OH. You might never go back to the mac-n-cheese in a box after trying this dish!

1 Preheat oven to 350°.
In a large bowl, combine the cheeses, dry mustard, worcestershire sauce, salt, cayenne pepper and pepper (optional nutmeg). Set aside. Place 1 cup milk and the heavy cream in a medium saucepan over low heat. Warm until it begins to steam, stirring occasionally. Do not boil.

2 In a measuring cup, mix 1/2 cup of milk with the tablespoon of cornstarch and stir until dissolved. Add to the milk and heavy cream mixture, constantly stir and bring to a boil for one minute. Remove from heat. Pour this mixture into bowl with cheeses and allow the cheese to melt.

3 Fill a large saucepan with water and place over high heat. Bring to a boil. Add a dash of salt and the pasta. Cook according to the directions on the package. Drain, add pasta to melted cheese mixture and mix. Pour into a large oven-safe dish. Mixture will be slightly soupy. Bake at 350° for 20-30 minutes or until it bubbles around the edge of the dish. Remove from oven and allow to sit for 5 minutes before serving.

TIP from Katie! You can sprinkle the top with some bread crumbs. Simply mix one cup of bread crumbs with two tablespoons of olive oil and sprinkle on top before cooking.

Cheesy Chicken Casserole

Serves 4

INGREDIENTS

2 chicken breasts
1 tablespoon butter
1 cup celery – chopped
1/4 cup yellow onion
   – chopped
2 cups broccoli florets
1/4 cup mayonnaise
4 ounces cream cheese
   – softened

1/3 cup chicken stock
Old Bay® seasoning
   to taste
salt/pepper to taste
2 cups plain potato chips
   – smashed
2 cups cheddar cheese
   – shredded

This was one of my recipes for a Comfort Foods class and the parents and students raved about it!

1 Preheat oven to 350°.
Place a large frying pan over medium heat. Season chicken pieces with salt and pepper. When frying pan is warm, add 1 tablespoon of butter, coating the bottom of the pan. Allow the butter to brown and add the chicken. Cook for one minute and stir meat around so that all sides are cooked, a total of 4 minutes. Remove from heat, place in a large bowl.

2 Add celery, onion, broccoli, mayonnaise, cream cheese and chicken stock to the chicken and mix with a spoon. Season with Old Bay®, salt and pepper.
Place in a casserole dish.

3 Sprinkle with cheddar cheese and smashed potato chips. Bake for 25 minutes or until cheese is melted and the chicken salad is bubbling.

 **TIP from Katie!** Have fun with this recipe by adding different vegetables, top it off with flavored potato chips and try various types of cheese!

Experiment! · How about a different cheese? · Be Creative!

Have Fun with it! · Season, Taste, Season, Taste. · What do you like?

Pasta

Pasta is one of the most incredible food products in the world because it is made from simple ingredients, it is inexpensive to produce, it is easy to store and it can be prepared quickly and easily, in a number of different ways.

Many people believe that pasta originated in Italy because pasta is such a staple in Italian cuisine but the history of pasta dates back as far as Ancient Greece and Rome. Several ethnic and cultural groups claim they "created" pasta including the Chinese, North Africans and the Italians. Marco Polo was said to have brought "noodles" back from China to Italy. These noodles were probably made from rice or breadfruit instead of wheat. The North Africans occupied southern Italy and many believe they brought with them a dried form of pasta. Pasta flourished in Italy because the climate was perfect for growing the hard durum wheat that semolina flour is made from and in turn made into pasta. The Sicilians are known to have first made dried pasta into tube shapes. The addition of tomato sauce did not come until after Columbus discovered the New World (15th Century) and brought the tomato back to Europe. One thing that can be said for certain is that pasta is represented in some form or another in many cuisines around the world.

FUN FACT : North Dakota is known for growing over 70% of the durum wheat grown in the United States and it is exported all over the world, even to Italy.

Facts:

Pasta is divided into two basic categories, dried and fresh. Dried pasta is made from flour and water while fresh pasta has the addition of eggs. Pasta is traditionally made from durum wheat. This wheat produces flour called semolina and it is high in gluten. Gluten is a protein found in flour, which gives it structure. Pasta holds its shape and will not fall apart when boiled because the gluten strands are bound together.

Pasta comes in many different shapes and sizes. There are several different flavors of pasta as well. Spinach, beet juice, lemons and herbs can impart flavor and color into pasta for a different taste and texture. Some pasta is served with a sauce (spaghetti), some is layered in a dish (lasagna), while others are stuffed (ravioli, tortellini and cannelloni).

Here are some recommendations about pasta uses:

- *Small shapes ~ soups*
- *Thin strand pasta ~ with light sauces*
- *Broad strands, tubes or large shapes ~ thick and meaty sauces*
- *Large hollow shapes/tubes or wide sheets ~ layered or filled baked dishes*

The basic process of making pasta involves combining the flour with either water or egg. Mechanical action is applied and the dough is worked into a tough ball, which is a result of working the gluten. The pasta is then either rolled out and cut or it is put through a machine that will create the desired shape.

Preparation and Care: *Cooking pasta properly is very important.*

1. First, one must coordinate the timing of the sauce and the boiling of the pasta.

2. Cook pasta in a large pot filled with plenty of water. This is very important so that the pasta will cook evenly and not stick together. The recommended ratio is 4 quarts of water for every pound of pasta. The water should be brought to a rapid boil before adding the pasta.

3. Add one or two tablespoons of salt to the boiling water before adding all of the pasta.

4. Stir the pasta with a wooden spoon while waiting for the water to re-boil. When this occurs, turn the heat down slightly. Begin timing according to the directions on the pasta package. Stir the pasta frequently. Fresh pasta typically takes 2-7 minutes, depending on the size and thickness while dried pasta typically cooks for 8-10 minutes. Dried pasta is best cooked "al dente". This is the Italian phrase for "with a bite", which means it should not be over-cooked and mushy.

5. Drain immediately in a colander in the sink. The pasta will begin to dry out and stick together if it is left in the colander for more than 5 minutes, which is why it is important to have your sauce ready. If your sauce is not ready, transfer hot pasta to a bowl and drizzle with about 1 tablespoon of olive oil to help keep it from sticking.

When cooking filled pasta, like ravioli, a more gentle cooking approach should be applied so that the filling will not fall out. The water should be at a calm boil and it should be carefully stirred. Filled pasta is usually ready to be removed when they begin to float to the top. Use a slotted spoon instead of a colander to remove filled pasta from the hot water.

If pasta is being used for a cold application like pasta salad, the pasta should be "shocked" immediately after it is drained by rinsing it under cold water. This will stop the pasta from cooking and will cool the pasta down quickly.

Storing pasta varies depending on whether it is dried or fresh. Dried pasta will last in a sealed box or bag for up to 2 months. If it is kept in an airtight container away from heat, moisture and light this can be extended to 1 year. Fresh pasta must be refrigerated or frozen. It will last 3 days in the refrigerator and 1 month in the freezer. It should be wrapped well in plastic wrap to prevent exposure to moisture.

FUN FACT:

It is estimated that each kid in the US eats 62 pounds of pasta per year. This is more than any other age group. Typically the pasta is in the form of spaghetti or macaroni & cheese.

Nutrition:

Pasta is a good source of carbohydrate, is low in fat and is a low sodium food. Many varieties of pasta will also provide a good source of fiber, protein and vitamin B. With the addition of a vitamin rich tomato sauce, a small plate of pasta can be a delicious and nutritious meal.

Chicken Noodle Soup

Serves 4

INGREDIENTS

2 chicken breasts – cut into bite size pieces

1/3 cup yellow onion – large chopped

1 medium carrot – large chopped

1 celery stalk – large chopped

2 tablespoons butter – divided

1 bay leaf

1/2 teaspoon dried oregano or thyme

6 cups chicken stock or broth

1 cup small pasta or 2 cups egg noodles

salt/pepper to taste

Everyone should know how to make chicken noodle soup. Once you make it from scratch, you will not go back to soup in a can!

Place a 4 quart saucepan over medium heat. Season chicken pieces with salt and pepper. When saucepan is warm, add 1 tablespoon butter coating the bottom of the pan. Allow the butter to brown and add the chicken. Cook for one minute and then stir meat around so that all sides are cooked, a total of 4 minutes. Remove from heat, place in a large bowl and set aside.

Replace 4 quart saucepan over medium low heat and wait until it is warm. Add 1 tablespoon of butter and allow it to melt. Add the chopped onion, carrot, celery, bay leaf and dried herbs. Sauté until vegetables are soft, about 3 minutes.

Add the 6 cups of chicken stock or broth and bring to a boil. Add the pasta and simmer for 10 minutes. Add the chicken and simmer for another 10 minutes. Season with salt and pepper. Serve warm.

Once you know this basic soup recipe you can try different meats, vegetables and pastas!

Pasta Primavera Salad

Serves 6

INGREDIENTS

2 cups bowtie, penne or rainbow spiral pasta
1 tablespoon salt
2 cups broccoli florets – blanched
20 snow peas or snap peas
1 medium carrot – grated
1/4 cup red onion – small chopped
15 cherry or grape tomatoes
    – cut in half, lengthwise

VINAIGRETTE

1 tablespoon shallots – minced
1 teaspoon garlic – minced
2 teaspoons Dijon mustard
2 tablespoons red wine vinegar
    or lemon juice

dash of Tabasco®
1/2 cup olive oil
salt/pepper to taste

It is a meal in itself!

1 Fill a 4 quart saucepan with water and place over high heat. Bring to a boil. Place broccoli in a strainer and dip into boiling water for 30 seconds. Remove strainer and run broccoli under cold water. Drain and place into a large bowl.

2 Bring water to a boil again and add 1 tablespoon of salt and the pasta. Stir the pasta with a wooden spoon while waiting for the water to re-boil. When this occurs, turn the heat down slightly. Begin timing according to the directions on the pasta package. Stir the pasta frequently.

3 Snap off the top of each pea pod and pull down the length of the pod to remove tough string. Place them along with the grated carrot and chopped red onion in the large bowl with the broccoli.

4 In a small bowl, whisk together the shallots, garlic, mustard, vinegar or lemon juice and Tabasco®. Slowly add the olive oil while whisking. Season with salt and pepper. Set aside.

5 Drain pasta and "shock" it by running cold water over it to stop the cooking process. Add the pasta to the bowl of vegetables and add the vinaigrette. Mix together, taste it and adjust seasoning if necessary. Add the tomatoes and gently mix. Refrigerate for at least 1 hour and serve cold.

TIP from Katie! Reserve 1/4 cup of the vinaigrette and just before serving add it to the pasta salad to "liven" it up!

Apple Almond Raisin Couscous

Serves 6

INGREDIENTS

1 cup apple juice
1/4 teaspoon salt
2 tablespoons butter
  – divided
1 cup dry couscous
1/3 cup raisins
1 apple – peeled, cored
  and cut into cubes
1/4 teaspoon cinnamon

1/3 cup almonds
  – sliced and
  toasted
1 tablespoon honey
1 tablespoon olive oil
salt/pepper to taste

This recipe was inspired by a dish from a Dinner Party Project where 7th & 8th graders made dinner for 25 senior citizens in Brookline, MA. It was a hit!!

1 In a large saucepan, combine apple juice, 1 tablespoon butter and 1/4 teaspoon salt. Bring to a boil. Remove from heat, add couscous and raisins. Stir well, cover and let stand for 5 minutes (or as long as directed on the package of couscous).

2 Place a small frying pan over medium heat. When the pan is warm, add 1 tablespoon butter, the apple cubes and sprinkle with cinnamon. Sauté for 2 minutes. Set aside.

3 Remove lid from couscous and fluff using a fork. Add the sautéed apples, almonds, honey, olive oil and mix. Season with salt and pepper, taste, adjust seasoning and serve warm.

TIP from Katie! Unable to find toasted, sliced almonds. Place untoasted sliced almonds in a toaster oven on 350° for 5 minutes. Set a timer because nuts toast quickly and can burn easily!

Baked Ziti

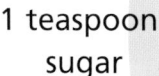

Serves 6

INGREDIENTS

1 pound ground beef
2 tablespoons olive oil
1 shallot – chopped
1 tablespoon garlic – minced
2 teaspoons dried basil
1 teaspoon dried oregano
1 (28 ounce) can of
   crushed/peeled tomatoes

1 teaspoon
   sugar
2 cups shredded cheese
   mixture
   (e.g. mozzarella, parmesan,
   asiago, provolone)
3 cups pasta – ziti
salt/pepper to taste

This is a hearty meal, best served with a salad and some bread. It can easily be reheated and usually tastes better the second day!

1 Place a large frying pan over medium high heat. When pan is very warm, add the ground beef, breaking up meat with a spatula as it browns. Cook until it is no longer pink. Drain any excess fat and place cooked beef in a large bowl and set aside.

2 Place the large frying pan over medium heat and add the oil. When the oil is hot, add the shallot, garlic, dried herbs and sauté for 1-2 minutes. Add the entire can of tomatoes and season with the sugar and salt and pepper. Simmer on low heat for 15 minutes. Pour sauce into the bowl with ground beef and add 1 cup of the cheese. Mix together.

3 Preheat oven to 350°.
Fill a 4 quart saucepan with water and place over high heat. When water begins to boil, add 1 tablespoon of salt and the pasta. Stir the pasta with a wooden spoon while waiting for the water to re-boil. When this occurs, turn the heat down slightly. Begin timing according to the directions on the pasta package. Stir the pasta frequently.

4 Drain pasta, place in large bowl with the sauce/meat/cheese mixture and mix together. Place in an oven safe dish and sprinkle remaining cheese on top. Bake for 15 minutes or until it begins to bubble. Let stand for 10 minutes before serving.

48 pasta

TIP **from Katie!** Feel free to substitute ground turkey or chicken for the beef to create a different flavor!

Chicken & Veggies over Pasta

Serves 4

INGREDIENTS

2 boneless chicken breasts
   – cut into bite size pieces
juice of one lemon
2 cups dried pasta
1/2 tablespoon butter
1/4 cup onion – small chopped
(scallions, shallots or Spanish onion)
1 tomato – large chopped

2 cups mixed fresh
   vegetables
(e.g. broccoli, cauliflower, green
beans, red pepper, squash)
2 tablespoons & 1 teaspoon
   olive oil
*Optional: grated Parmesan
cheese*

This is a quick and delicious meal – no side dishes needed!

1 Place chicken pieces in a small bowl and cover with lemon juice. Mix to coat and then let sit for 20 minutes.

2 Fill a 4 quart saucepan with water and place over high heat. When water begins to boil, add 1 tablespoon of salt and the pasta. Stir the pasta with a wooden spoon while waiting for the water to re-boil. When this occurs, turn the heat down slightly. Begin timing according to the directions on the pasta package. Stir the pasta frequently. Drain pasta, add 1 teaspoon of olive oil and coat pasta. Place in serving bowls.

3 While the pasta is cooking, place a large frying pan over medium high heat. Season lemon marinated chicken pieces with salt and pepper. When pan is very warm, add the butter, allowing it to turn brown and then add the chicken. Sear chicken on all sides for about 3 minutes. Reduce heat to medium low and add the onions and tomato, cook for 1 minute.

4 Add 2 tablespoons olive oil and the rest of the vegetables to the large frying pan. Stir, season with salt and pepper and then cover with a lid. Cook for about 3 minutes stirring occasionally. Serve over pasta and sprinkle with cheese.

TIP from Katie! Head to the salad bar and choose already prepared vegetables to make this recipe even easier. Also, have fun using different marinades for the chicken.

Your Pasta Recipe Page

Experiment! · Make it the way you like it! · Try something new.

Mix things up! · What's your favorite vegetable? · Share your ideas!